FIBER ARTS ENFOLDS
KWANZAA
QUILTS AND ZAWADI DOLLS

African American Quilt and Doll Guild

Warrensville Heights, Ohio

December 2020

Gloria Allen Kellon

Barbara Freeman Eady, Editors

Photography, Patricia Fantroy

Cover Quilt, Kwanzaa by Helen Murrell

Dedication & Acknowledgments

This book is crammed with the hopes, dreams and talents of a group of women and one man who reached up and out to let their souls fly with the creativity they knew was within. This fiber arts project is dedicated to all of the members of the African American Quilt and Doll Guild who pulled together to showcase some of our artwork.

Aknowledgements
Over the years many have inspired, helped, taught, and encouraged us along the way. We will always be grateful for your support. We scatter stars of honor at your feet.

Dr. Carolyn L. Mazloomi
Artist, Quilter, Independent Curator, Author, WCQN
Bess Lomax Hawes NEA National Heritage Fellow
***
Kyra E. Hicks
"How to Self-Publish Your Own Quilt Catalog"
Quilter, Author, Quilt Historian
***
Dolls Like Us
Cleveland, Detroit, Chicago
***
Linda Goss, Poet, Co-Founder
National Association of Black Storytellers
NEA National Heritage Fellow
***
Anna Arnold, Director
The Florence O'Donnell Wasmer Gallery
Ursuline College
***
Margaret Simon, Public Relations Manager
Shaker Heights Public Library
***
Barbara Eady
Quilt Artist, Graphics
***
Sandra Noble

Quilt Artist, Art Consultant

Preface

A dream realized, is one of the most phenomenal and amazing gifts of life. As happenstance would have it, two African American fabric-lovers met in a local fabric store. As friends they began talking about the fact that they should have "their own" guild and acting on this issue, Sandra Noble and Gloria Kellon decided to call the first meeting of the African American Quilt and Doll Guild. In April, 2006 at the Warrensville Civic and Senior Center cloth doll makers, quilters, crafters, and those interested gathered. An African American guild had life. Fourteen years and 65 members later, this group has undergone a world of experiences in quilting, dollmaking, teaching, and friendship. The goals are to learn skills, research the history of African and African American textiles and those gifted artists of yesterday and today who mastered the needle and the fabric.

AAQDG gives to the life of our communities by teaching classes, giving displays and lectures on quilting and African American history. Narrative quilts of this guild are traveling the world telling our stories. Fourteen members traveled to South Africa to celebrate the life of Nelson Mandela.

Through the years, many friends of quilting, such as Dr. Carolyn Mazloomi, a Bess Lomax Hawes NEA National Heritage Fellow has encouraged and inspired us along the way.

AAQDG has supported African American quilt artists by inviting them to hold workshops in our meetings. Bisa Butler, Rachel Clark, Carolyn Cump, Juanita Yaeger as well as doll artists, Kooki Davis and Pamela Turner have shared their expertise.

Fourteen years later, we are still stitching, learning, and teaching inspite of the changes in life brought on by a pandemic, racism, political wars, and economic stress. Quilts are now our effective way of improving civil rights for all in America. Quilts are the silent stitches which tell the whole story.

Gloria Kellon

Foreward

A few years ago, the African American Quilt and Doll Guild of Warrensville Heights, Ohio published a book highlighting the creative and unique fiber works produced by the quilters and doll makers in the guild.

This, the second book published by the guild has a focus on Kwanzaa, an African American tradition. As a guild of predominantly African Americans members, we acknowledge and celebrate the traditions of our history and culture. Many of the quilts and dolls that were created reflect our interpretations of African American history and culture.

For the last five years at their annual Christmas holiday luncheon, members of the AAQDG participated in an interactive program celebrating Kwanzaa. A traditional Kwanzaa table is set up with items donated by different members. A woven mat called the mkeka covers the table along with the kinara, a handmade candleholder which holds the seven black, green, and red candles in the center of the mat. The Unity Cup, dried fruit and vegetables are added. Ears of dried corn represent the "watoto" the children of our families. Children are the future. A small handmade item or a special book representing creativity and Education are not forgotten.

For the program, selected guild members read the descriptions of each of the seven principles of Kwanzaa to reinforce our knowledge. Lastly, we give and receive gifts from each other.

Our guild is a reflection of the principles of Kwanzaa because we follow many of the principles during our recourse of meeting together, learning from each other, and skillfully producing quilts and dolls.

It was a natural outcome of our Kwanzaa activities that Gloria Kellon, a co-founder of the guild challenged the members to create quilts and dolls to commemorate Kwanzaa. The beautiful and well-crafted quilts, dolls and other items created by the guild members in this book are the result of the Kellon challenge.

Sandra Noble

Table of Contents

PRAISE SONG FOR KWANZAA!

MY BELLS ARE RINGING!
MY SOUL IS SINGING!
WELL, O WELL, WELL! IT'S KWANZAA TIME!

CALL YOUR FATHER!
CALL YOUR MOTHER!
CALL YOUR SISTER!
CALL YOUR BROTHER!

IT'S KWANZAA TIME. FAMILY TIME!
IT'S KWANZAA TIME. FAMILY TIME!

BLACK PEOPLE COMING TOGETHER-- HARAMBEE!
TRYING TO MAKE THINGS BETTER-- HARAMBEE!

SEVEN DAYS AND SEVEN NIGHTS
SEVEN CANDLES WE WILL LIGHT.
SEVEN CANDLES WE WILL LIGHT.

IT'S KWANZAA TIME. FAMILY TIME!
IT'S KWANZAA TIME. FAMILY TIME!

Mama Linda Goss

Kwanzaa Quilts & Zawadi Dolls

All quilts have stories to tell. Quilts bring comfort whether sick or well at any time and in any place. Quilts are beautiful to see and are often treasured even when worn and tattered. Narrative quilts are soothing as well as entertaining. Their stories play to the imagination or the unique tale stitched with patient love. Art quilts represent an artform which expresses love of needlecrafts as well addiction to fabric. The patchwork reminds us of days gone by and loved ones who spent time creating family treasures. The stitched cloth tells a silent story which in today's world often teaches or promotes an idea. Art quilts have acquired a voice. This voice captures the unsuspecting quilt viewer and leads to a change of opinion or a positive action. Some of these stories are of the celebration of Kwanzaa as well as the celebration of life.

Kwanzaa quilt stories are African American family stories. Through the medium of fiber art, members of the African American Quilt and Doll Guild turned to needle and thread to stitch these narratives using the imagination and unique techniques. The word zawadi means gift. Throughout these pages, the theme of Sankofa will flow in the designs of the artists. Sankofa, an African word which means "learn about the past, in order to make good decisions for the future" is symbolized by a mythical bird looking backward. The quilts and dolls in this book are sharing the meaning of Kwanzaa through quilts and dolls in honoring the family, community, nation, and race.

Also included are quilts which mark the historical journey of the fight for civil rights. Our heroes and sheroes are highlighted by the art of the quilt and the doll. Perhaps you will want to make a quilt to share the joy of Kwanzaa or your special days.

In African customs and culture, Kwanzaa is a celebration of the Harvest or "First Fruits" that comes after the hard work has been done!

Kwanzaa is a Kiswahili word meaning "first fruits." After the season of working to produce constructive end results, workers look forward with pride and self-satisfaction to the celebration and thanksgiving. The plan of the past year is assessed and new plans are made. Kwanzaa is an African American cultural week of gathering family and friends, renewing commitments, and community sharing. In celebrating African and African American music, poetry, history, art, and literature is saturated into the celebrating throughout the Kwanzaa days in order to teach the young and to remind adults to live more positive lives in the New Year. Knowledge of the history of African-American people, their individual family genealogy, their struggle for equal rights, our heroes and sheroes are also honored. The principles of Kwanzaa inspire and reinforce those dreams and creativity for enriching each life in the next season.

Kwanzaa was developed by Dr. Maulana Karenga in the sixties to bring the African American diaspora together and to give them hope, unity and direction. During this time, there was a struggle for civil rights in the United States and in many parts of the world. The celebration of Kwanzaa helped pull people together. This is called Harambee.

Kwanzaa begins on the first day after Christmas from December 26th through December 31st. Each night a candle is lit and its meaning is discussed in the family or community gathering. There will be appropriate stories, poems, or music in the family circles. The Nguzo Saba is the statement of values which are the guides and the embodiment of the celebration.

Nguzo Saba
The Seven Principles

Umoja
(Unity)

To strive for and maintain unity in the family, community, nation and race.

Kujichagulia
(Self-Determination)

To define ourselves, name ourselves, create for ourselves and speak for ourselves.

Ujima
(Collective Work and Responsibility)

To build and maintain our community together and make our brother's and sister's problems our problems and to solve them together.

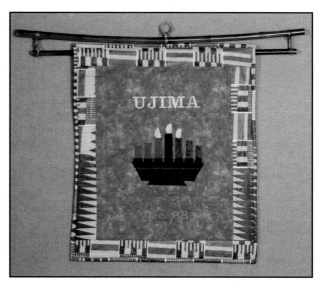

Ujamaa
(Cooperative Economics)

To build and maintain our own stores, shops,
and other businesses and to
profit from them together.

Nia
(Purpose)

To make our collective vocation the building
and developing of the community in order to
restore our people to their traditional greatness.

Kuumba
(Creativity)

To do always as much as we can,
in the way we can, in order to leave
our community more beautiful
than we inherited it.

Imani
(Faith)

To believe with all out heart
in our people, our parents, teachers,
our leaders and the righteousness and
victory of our struggle.

Nguzo Saba quilts by Jacqueline Boyd

Quilts and Kwanzaa

Part of the joy of the Kwanzaa celebration is the preparation and decoration for these seven important days. Each day has the greeting "Habari gani?" with the response of the name of the day of Kwanzaa.

A small table will be set for use during Kwanzaa week. The table will contain important and significant items for the celebration. Books and Art pieces are welcomed here. The table should be covered with a cloth which may be the colors of black, red, or green which are the colors of Kwanzaa. Traditional African mudcloth, Kuba cloth, Korhogo cloth, or other cotton textiles of the Motherland may be used. This display recognizes our African roots by including African Art pieces, African baskets and Adinkra symbols. This use of textiles gives an opportunity for large and small quilts, or table runners with a Kwanzaa theme to be a part of the celebration.

There are Adinkra symbols which represent the principles off Kwanzaa. This system of symbols represents words and ideas, and is the unspoken language of Adinkra symbols. These symbols convey high moral ideals, honor and respect. In Ghana and other countries on the west coast of Africa, the symbols are used to embellish fabric, clothing, buildings, in jewelry and are used in day to day events.

The Kwanzaa table should contain:

1. Mazao (the crops) Ear s of corn, sweet potatoes, apples
2. Mkeka (the mat) The mat should be woven of a natural fiber.
3. Kinara (the candleholder) A wooden carved kinara is suggested
4. Muhindi (Ears of corn)
5. Mishumaa saba (the seven candles)
   Three red, one black, and three green are needed.
6. Kikombe cha umoja (the unity cup)
   This is a special handcrafted cup.
7. Zawadi (gifts) Gifts should be handmade or could a promise or a new goal.

Two additional items for the table:
   Bendera (flag) Black, Red, Green
   Nguzo Saba (A Seven Principles Poster)

The table covering and the Nguzo Saba Poster lead the creative quilter to imagine opportunities for their craft. The makeka or mat on the table represents the African culture and history. It is the foundation for this special setting. The kinara is placed next on the mat. The kinara is a candle-holder which represents our ancestors and the continuance of our people. The muhinidi, ears of corn represent the children (watoto) and all of the hopes and dreams for the children. Our children are the hope for the future. There should be an ear of corn for each child in the family or children you want to be in the family. Pictures of those who work daily for better laws and equal rights in our lives are put on display.

The seven candles are lit in the kinara one day at a time in a specific order. As you face the table, on the left are 3 red candles, in the center one black candle, then 3 green candles. On the first day of Kwanzaa the black candle representing Umoja (unity} is lit. The other candles are lit one day at a time with discussion and consideration about the meaning of the principle of the day.

The unity cup (kikombe cha umoja) is used to pour libation to honor the ancestors and to set the feeling of Unity by drinking from a common cup. In libation, as water is poured (in a plant or on the earth), names are called out of those ancestors revered in a family and in our history. In family ceremonies, families reinforce unity by sharing the Unity cup.

Zawadi, gifts are placed on the table. Gifts are handmade or of a nature which shows that the principles are in mind. Gifts are mainly for the children. Books are acceptable gifts to emphasize learning. Children often give promised gifts of actions to their parents, such as being helpful around the house, studying harder at school, or practicing more on music instruments.

The Karamu

On the last day of Kwanzaa, a culmination of the entire week is held. All of the family and friends gather.

The Quilter and Kwanzaa

The timelessness of quilts and the beauty of African textiles together with principles of Kwanzaa inspires one to create a quilt for this family occasion. Quilts have been used for many purposes for thousands of years throughout the world. Research has found quilts were used as shields to protect the horses of ancient African horsemen. Quilted clothing was worn in China for warmth and comfort from medieval times.

Quilts can be used as table coverings for the Kwanzaa feast called the Karamu on the last day of Kwanzaa. Beautiful quilted table runners would add to the festivities of this occasion. The Karamu table on the last day of Kwanzaa with its food-laden grandeur would be complimented by beautiful runners, and the grand African dress is worn on this occasion with their colorful Kwanzaa themes. The Kwanzaa runners would enhance the array of soul food and favorite dishes.

Textile-lovers are always able to find a way to use fabric as a "building material" for their projects. In today's world with the abundance of stabilizers, fusibles and beautiful threads, suggests a myriad of items which could be constructed for Kwanzaa using textiles.

Some suggestions are:

1. Tablecloths
2. Table runners
3. Poster-size Quilts
4. Door Decorations
5. Kwanzaa Dolls
6. Fabric Bowls
7. Pillow Covers or Cushions
8. Fabric Book Jackets
9. Fabric Totes and Purses

My Kwanzaa Table

The making of my Kwanzaa quilt brought to mind my mother's creativity in setting our dinner table. There was the proper placement of plates, glasses, flatware and the delicious meals. There was designated seating and pieces of fried chicken – the younger siblings getting the legs with socks. My dad always stressed the importance of being together as a family, so the dinner time gathering was mandatory.

Inside those memories of my childhood table, I see a reflection of the Kwanzaa table. For the seven-day celebration of Kwanzaa, items that have meaning and purpose like the Muhindi and the Kinara holding Mishumaa, are carefully placed. Each day the family gathers to light a candle and answer the question, Habari Gani? (What's the news!). The answer or news for the day is presented as a principle and family members share ideas for its attainment. At my family dinner table, candles were usually saved for holidays or for when my parents would try to have a romantic meal without us. Topics of conversation were generally about school, work and whose turn it was to do the dishes. Even when those conversations seemed combative the solution was always constructive. Looking back and even then, I realize the intent was always to nurture and encourage us to be our best selves in life.

I hope you are inspired to create a Kwanzaa table this year.

Title: "My Kwanzaa Table"
Measurements: 52" X 44"
Date Created: 2017
Materials: Cottons, batiks and sequined fabric rattan cotton silk and monofilament thread
Artist: Felecia Tinker
Quilted by: Norma Dixon

Felecia Tinker

Kwanzaa – The Family Celebration

Kwanzaa is celebrated by the family in this quilt. The family is dressed in their finest representation of African clothing. The family has a beautiful tablecloth and mat with all of the symbols of the celebration. The table holds corn representing children and fruits of the harvest.

The seven candles in the colors of red, green and black have been placed in a candle holder called a kinara.

The black candle represents Umoja – Unity, and is lit on the first day of Kwanzaa. It is placed in the middle of the kinara. The red candles are placed to the left of the black candle and the green candles are placed to the right of the black candle.

The red candles represent the principles: Kujichagulia - Self-determination, Ujima, Cooperative Economics, and Kuumba – Creativity.

The green candles represent the principles: Ujamaa – Collective Work and Responsibility, Nia – Purpose, and Imani – Faith.

Title: "Kwanzaa - The Family Celebration"
Materials: commercial cottons, beads
Techniques: original design, piecing raw edge applique
Date Created: December 2016
Artist Carolyn Baker Jenkins

Carolyn Baker Jenkins

The Unity Cup – Kikombe Cha Umoja
The Unity Cup is used during the Kwanzaa
Celebration to pour libation to the ancestors in
remembrance and honor of those who paved the
path down which we walk and who taught us the
good and beauty in life.

Title: "The Unity Cup – Kikombe Cha Umoja"
Matrials: Commercial Cottons, Beads
Techniques: Original Design, Raw Edge Applique
Date Created: September 9, 2017
Artist: Carolyn Baker Jenkins

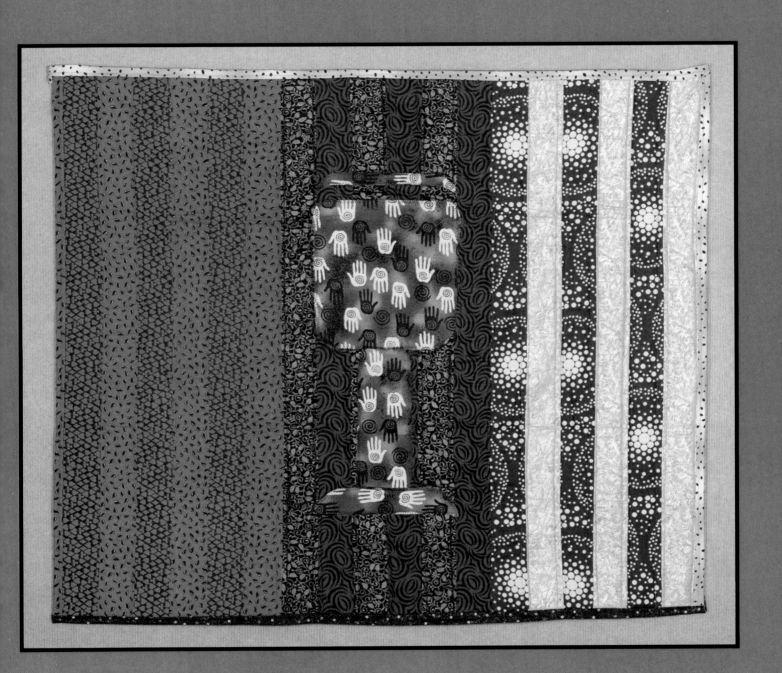

Kwanzaa Way of Life

I came of age when Kwanzaa was introduced, and expanded my horizons by moving to New York City. My appreciation for self-realization was heightened by becoming an adult in that international environment. I have formal training in design, and a family legacy of uplifting the community. Talents are used to positively impact economic well-being either by production, informed consumerism, committing a percentage of purchasing from my people, or paying it forward. My family does not limit the lifestyle to that week after Christmas. We are not religious, but we celebrate our joy in each other and our best wishes for all humanity.

Our way of expressing these seven principles is by our daily approach to living. Whenever possible, everything is purchased on sale. Conspicuous consumption is generally avoided. My quilt is a banner for sharing with the next generations my political, cultural and economic way of doing things. All materials are from the stash I had already purchased. Some textiles are remnants, while others, like the Kwanzaa print of the background, were in the stash waiting for a purpose. The covered button forms displaying the 7 principles and the upholstery fringe at the bottom were all among the retrieved items in my personal "store" of materials that were taking up space at home. Creative frugality is seen as a virtue rather than an economic necessity because the pride of producing outweighs the necessity to watch the budget. This special project enabled me to recapture the money I had already spent – Economics 101!

Jakki Dukes

18

The Keepers

My Kwanzaa quilt celebrates my ancestors who were able to endure the journey. They were the ones who were the keepers of traditions, community, culture, love of family, and of Africa. All of the ancestors who came before me, are part of me, and in retrospect, I am really all of them.
38" X 34"

Carole Richburg Brown

A. B. Hart Project

My students created the fabric pieces in my Home Economics Classes. They had to sew by hand using basic running stitches and back stitches. The pattern was created from African symbols that I found in a book. They used iron-on crayons that were heat set by heat. They stitched the stitches with embroidery thread. The next step was to sew fabric on each side of the square.

Title: A. B. Hart Project
Materials: Fabric, iron-crayons, embroidery thread
Techniques: Any pattern backstitch and running stitch
Date Created: 2002 and February 2017
Artist: Casandra L. Brown

Casandra L. Brown

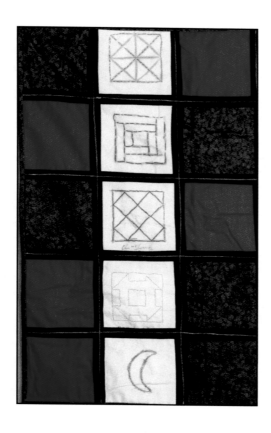

The Seven Principles of Kwanzaa: A Familty Ritual

The Seven Principles of Kwanzaa: A Family Ritual
My vision for this quilt design was to bring a sense of family into its meaning. The techniques I decided to use were silk screen, dye discharge, machine quilting and piecing. The materials are cotton front and back, cotton batting and beads.

Helen Murrell

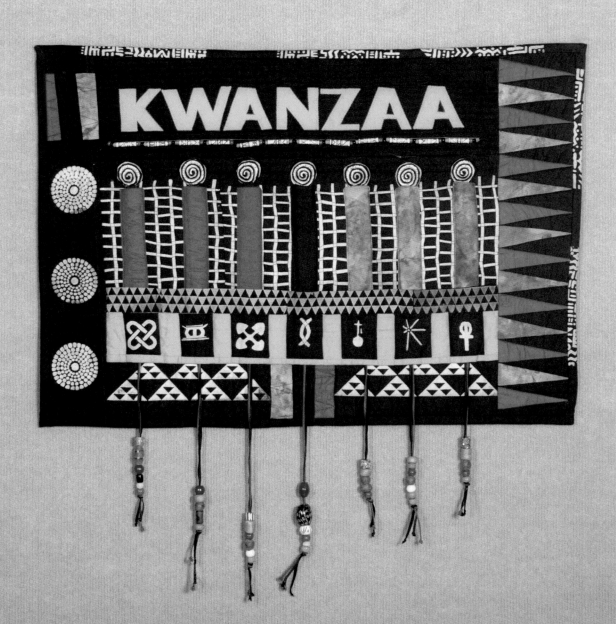

Kwanzaa

My husband, Steven Boyd, introduced me to Kwanzaa in 1983. He was a member of the Phoenix Black Theater Troupe (Phoenix, AZ) and they were hosting a community Kwanzaa celebration.

I was attracted to this holiday, Kwanzaa. It connected us, in the African Diaspora, to Africa. I was one of those "I'm Black and I'm Proud", afro wearing, fist pumping sistahs from the 70's. I always wanted to make a connection to my Motherland and I found this to be an uplifting, profound and spiritual way of doing just that.

Dr. Karenga incorporated aspects of the "first harvest" festivals (throughout Africa" and African philosophy with traditions and rituals that all African descendants could participate in regardless of your religion, present location or social status.

The seven principles I could embrace because I was already trying to be about these things. I loved the sound and feel of the Kiswahili words that were associated with the holiday: Habari Gani, Jambo, Kwa here, Asante sana, Harambee, etc. The seven principles: Umoja, Kujichagulia, Ujima, Ujamaa, Nia, Kuumba, and Imani. The seven symbols (represented on the Kwanzaa table) mkeka, kinara, nguzo saba, kikombe cha umoja, muhindi, mazoa and zawadi.

Since the beginning, we have annually participated on some level with public Kwanzaa celebrations here in Cleveland, Ohio. Gathering with the community and recognizing that millions of others throughout the African Diaspora were assembling and carrying out the same ceremony. I most enjoy our private family Kwanzaa... lighting of the candles, discussing the principles and how we will manifest them in the coming year. Libation and ancestor recognition gives us an opportunity to reflect on family stories, family history. Our son and now our granddaughters can feel connected to our grandparents, great-grandparents and other relatives that are no longer with us. I feel confident that my family will carry on this tradition in the years to come and my Kwanzaa Quilts will be an integral part.

Jacqueline Boyd

Courage

For nearly twenty years, our family has participated in the celebration of Kwanzaa. Coming after the Christian holiday of Christmas, it is the perfect holiday to spread some seeds of wisdom onto the young people of our family.

The seven principles of Kwanzaa and the understandings of each of them is invaluable. These principles are so helpful in the development of well-rounded individuals. Some of these principles seem so natural to me, such as Creativity and Faith.

This banner focuses on Purpose: Why am I here? What could I do? What should I do? Am I here to be of service? Is there greatness in me or am I here to assist someone else in their endeavors? To be clear, in just these thoughts alone, my thinking goes right to the Seven Principles.

Kwanzaa is a wonderful time to instill in our children all of the basic values of what our faith and culture should mean to them. This holiday emphasizes the need for the family structure and its importance. We look forward to this special time we have together. It is a time of Unity. We hope this spirit will last throughout the coming year.

We have to accept the fact that these principles will take courage. Therefore, I have to include courage with love in my heart more than once in the banner.

Julia Hutchinson

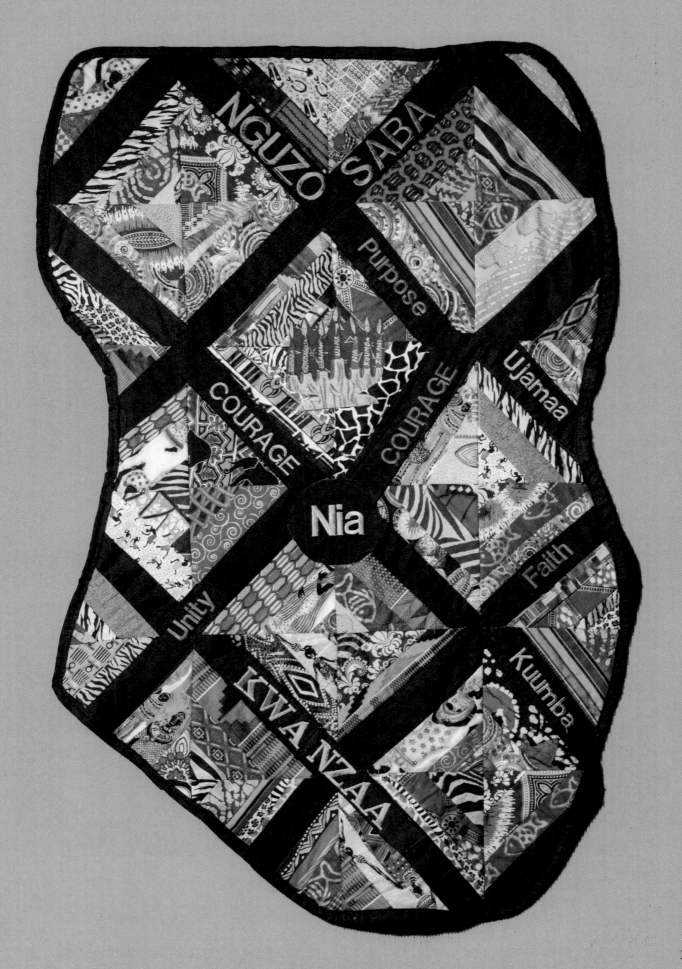

Happy Kwanzaa

In 1966, in the middle of the Civil Rights Movement, Dr. Maulana Karenga developed an idea which came to be called Kwanzaa. Through this holiday, African Americans could "connect" with their culture and their heritage. Today, celebrating this holiday beginning the day after Christmas and ending January 1, has become a tradition in many families world-wide. My quilt represents the seven candles, food, people and the image of the African continent signifying the African people or those who draw their heritage from Africa.

Title: Happy Kwanzaa
Materials: Cotton, Felt, Burlap, Fusible Webbing, Rayon Thread, Cotton Batting
Techniques: Embroidery, Machine Quilting, Double Diamond Ruler, Applique
Date Created: January, 2017
Artist Laura M. Croom

Laura M. Croom

I Am Woman

My adventures in doll making began with a trip to a sewing expo. I was mesmerized by a doll display that was put on by a local doll making group. I eventually became a member of that group and through many classes, workshops and help of fellow members I soon was creating my own special little people. I have always loved creating and doll making provides me with a path to do just that. Most of the creating come in the fashioning or costuming of the doll. By using special fabrics, fabric you make yourself. trims, beads and baubles you let your imagination go wild. Challenges come with the making of tiny parts such as fingers also the sculpting and painting of the faces. All of these take practice. The dolls that I create are mostly made with brown skin tones to reflect my heritage and to impress on the public that dolls of color are attractive and beautiful.

Mary Pinckney

Rosa Parks

When I was a little girl I loved playing with dolls. As the youngest child in my family, when everyone else was in school, the dolls were my friends and playmates. When I reached my teen years...no more dolls. But then when I was one year from retirement I went to the African American Quilt and Doll Guild Show and fell in love with dolls again. This time the dolls were created from cloth and patterns. I inquired whether I could buy a doll at the show, and was told, "No", but I was invited to join the guild where others would teach me to make my own dolls. Six months later I joined the Guild, bought my first sewing machine, and started on a new journey...learning to make dolls.

My challenges were many, from how to sew on a sewing machine to learning all of the doll making skills, including: selecting patterns, stuffing the dolls tightly, and drawing faces. The biggest challenges were building a stash of fabrics and threads, making the doll clothes, and finding the space in my house to work.

Now, my 40 plus dolls are all over the house. In fact they are taking over! Each doll has a story associated with it. I am especially proud of the dolls I made out of breast cancer fabric because they tell a special story of survival and are a constant reminder to me of my struggle and my strength.

I am so thankful that I was introduced to dollmaking and have begun to hone my craft because it has allowed me to learn a whole new set of skills, and because my number of friends has quadrupled.

Pamela E. Smith

African Queen

In all the years that I have been involved in dressmaking, crafts, quilting, and other needlework, I never considered doll making until I saw Kooki Davis' doll pattern. This African Queen doll called to me. I loved using the beautiful African fabrics, beads and other embellishments. The doll's simplicity to create, made it a joy to work with it as it grew stitch by stitch in front of me.

Bess Gates

Zawadi Doll

Years ago, collecting antique Black Dolls became a fascinating pastime of mine. I saw many historical horrors that were supposed to represent African American people. American manufacturers did not realize that there is a market for realistic and appropriate black dolls for our children. I decided to try my hand at the sewing machine which was new to me as well as to learn to follow a pattern. Gradually I imroved and now I am able to make a doll which would put a smile on a child's face. I enjoy looking for and recycling clothes that will fit and compliment the dolls. Doll making, not antique doll collecting is my new hobby.

Priscilla Bradley

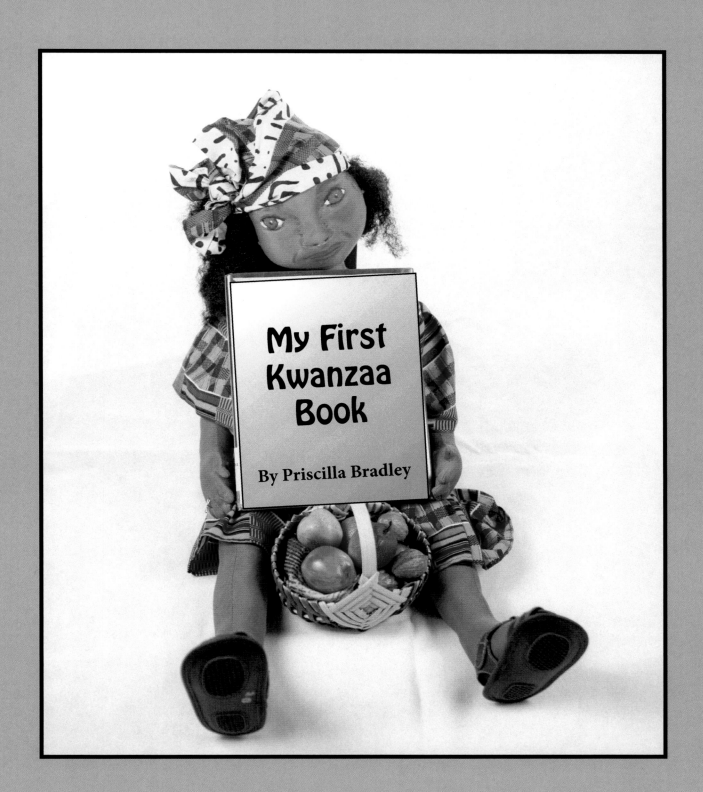

My First
Kwanzaa
Book

By Priscilla Bradley

IN PRAISE OF ANCESTOR CLOTH

By Mama Linda Goss

"Listen to the Ringing Bells!"
We wear the Stories We tell
And wrap them around our Souls.
Spinning, Stitching, Weaving Tales unfold.
Heavy, coarse, thin or soft
WE SING THE PRAISES
OF ANCESTOR CLOTHS.

Wrap me up
In MUDCLOTH.
Wrap me up
In MEMORY THREADS.
Wrap me up
In BARK CLOTH.
Wrap me up
In Mud...

I'm gonna
DANCE with my Story Cloth.
I'm gonna
DANCE all night long.
I'm gonna
DANCE with my Story Cloth.
DANCE 'til the mornin' comes.

INDIGO for my bed
A strip of that KENTE
For my head.

Wrap me up in MUDCLOTH.
KUBA around my feet.
GRANDMA'S QUILT draped
On my shoulders.
ADINKRA hugging my hips.
COWRIE SHELLS across my breast
A piece of that APPLIQUE
For my dress.

Wrap me up in KORHOGO ART.
Wrap me up in ADIRE PRINT.
Wrap me up in KANGA POEMS.
Wrap me up in Mud...

Wrap me up
in MUDCLOTH
Wrap me up
in PAPA SEEDS.
Wrap me up
in MAMA BEADS.
Wrap me up in Mud...

I'm gonna
DANCE with my Story Cloth.
I'm gonna
DANCE all day long.
I'm gonna
DANCE with my Story Cloth.
DANCE 'til the mornin' comes.

Kwanzaa Table Runner

Years ago I was in my first Kwanzaa celebration in a small rural community. I was amazed thab this holiday was so well-known there. The unity that was expressed was incredible. I started researching Kwanzaa and realized that I wanted to participate in this Afrocetric holiday. This table runner was created as a symbol for my household to honor the meaning of the Seven Principles and will be used in the years ahead for Kwanzaa time.

Allison Smith

Sheeley Kwanzaa Wall Hanging 2016

My familiarity with Kwanzaa was very limited, so the challenge to make a Kwanzaa item was exciting. I chose the quilt pattern called "Side Lights" by Kari Nichols of Mountainpeek Creations. The patterns allow the quilter to feature special fabrics and smaller blocks for just about anything you want to do.

Kwanzaa in the African American community is celebrated after the Christmas holiday. Kwanzaa addresses history, values, family, community and culture. The side blocks in the quilt highlight some of many values important to African American families and culture.

Title: Sheeley Kwanzaa Wall Hanging 2016
Materials: Cotton Fabrics, Polyester Threads
Techniques: Machine piecing with embroidery side blocks. Overall machine quilting.
Date Created: December 2016
Artist: Paulette C. Sheeley

Paulette C. Sheeley

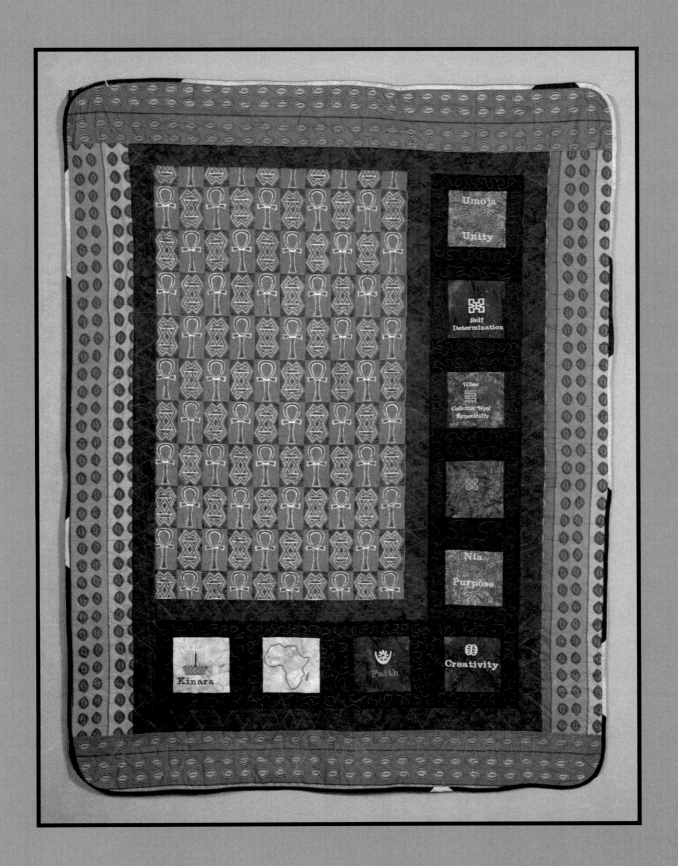

Lost Traditions

When I created this Kwanzaa quilt, I thought about the Africans who were torn from their homeland. They lost their families. They lost being a part of their community. They lost their traditions. They lost a sense of self. The tears on the quilt were for them.

As Africans came to the new land they came as slaves, no longer free men. People from other countries came as immigrants with family members, traditions and joy at coming to a new land.

The descendants of Africans in our country grew up with no true customs or rituals from past generations. Kwanzaa provided African Americans with a cultural connection to their African heritage. The principles of Kwanzaa: Umoja (Unity), Kujichagulia (Self-Determination), Ujima (Collective Work and Responsibility), Ujamaa (Cooperative Economics), Nia (Purpose), Kuumba (Creativity), and Imani (Faith) were combined with Adinkra symbols from the Ashanti Kingdom from Ghana. Both the principles and the symbols represent ways to live.

Sandra Noble – "Lost Traditions"
Year Made: 2005
Materials Used: Cotton fabric, gold trim, beads, pre-made letters

Sandra Noble

46

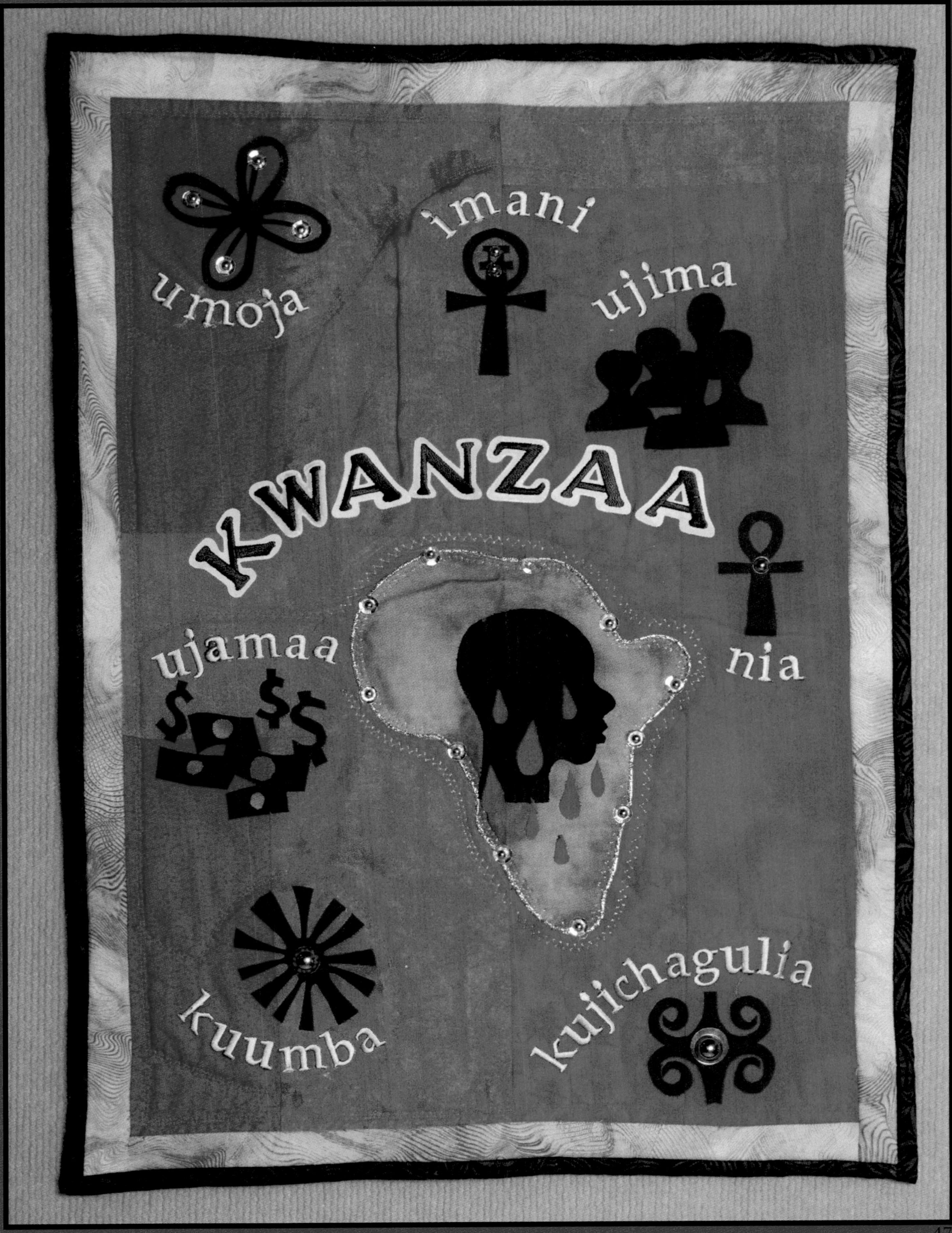
umoja
imani
ujima
KWANZAA
ujamaa
nia
kuumba
kujichagulia

"We live in turbulent times and our society seems rudderless. There is a need to strengthen and bring Back families together. Kwanzaa is a vehicle to achieve that. Each year families can review and renew a pledge to honor the principles of Kwanzaa. No matter what the age of family members, they can recognize how the principles can enhance and give direction for their way of life."

Title: Kwanzaa
Artist Sandra Noble
Year Made: 2016
Materials Used: Cotton Fabric, Inktense Pencils

Sankofa

As the celebration of Kwanzaa was practiced over the years in the homes and in the community, its acceptance made children and adults grow in pride and self-respect. The symbol of Kwanzaa is Sankofa symbolized by a mythical bird with its head looking back to the past to African American history. Knowing your history builds strength of character. Understanding positive principles of living develops attitudes which enable one to make better choices as the years go by.

Watching children in the classroom create Kwanzaa posters, cards, write poems, songs and create plays to teach others the meaning of the Kwanzaa principles was a thrilling experience for me. Their creativity taught others. In the early years of this holiday, many "staunch church-going grannies" came to the school programs to see if "these teachers" were teaching another religion. They soon understood and wanted the students' plays, poems and art to use themselves.

Title: Sankofa
Artist: Gloria A. Kellon
Size: 18" by 24"
Year: 2006
Materials: Cottons, machine embroidery,
           applique, batik fabric

Gloria A. Kellon

Kwanzaa Family Time

Umoja is a curious word whose true meaning might begin by exchanging jump ropes, lollipops, or signed contracts. It is a form of love and if it is sincere it is invaluable. In a family we may call unity, family ties and these ties are sealed in love. This quilt symbolizes a nuclear family but families come in all descriptions. The unity connections deepen over years of living. Unity in the family becomes unity in the community, our race, our city, and our country. UNITY can solve many problems.

Title: Kwanzaa Family Time
Artist: Gloria A. Kellon
Size: 18" by 24"
Year: 2016
Materials: Cotton, applique

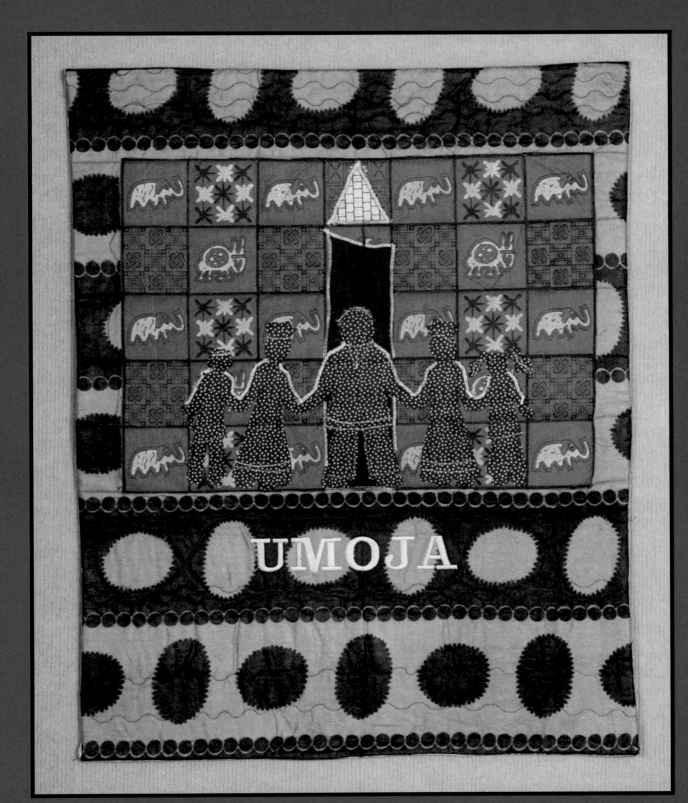

African Diaspora

In some ways, I believe quilting found me. As a graduate of Carnegie Mellon and Case Western Reserve Universities, I was busy developing my career goals. I held the position of Head Librarian of the Business Economics and Labor Department of the Cleveland Public Library. An outstanding quilt exhibit came to be displayed at the library and caught my attention. I was so intrigued that I found books and proceeded to experiment with this new craft. Since that time I have created many quilts and joined the AAQDG.

My most exciting achievement was the inclusion of the quilt entitled "My President" in the book Journey of Hope: Quilts Inspired by President Barack Obama by Dr. Carolyn Mazloomi. The quilt was exhibited at the National Afro-American Museum and Cultural Center in Wilberforce, Ohio. In 2009 this quilt was displayed in Yokohama, Japan when the President visited there. My recent quilts have been traveling the United State and South Africa. Exhibits included were: "And Still We Rise" and "Conscience of the Human Spirit."

Julius Bremer

Title: African Diaspora
Artist: Julius Bremer
Size: 31 X 34
Year: 2017
Materials: Cotton

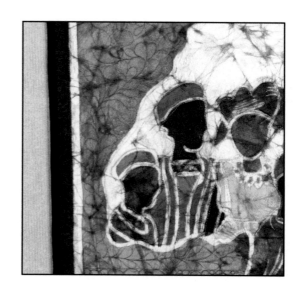

"One of the unique opportunities of quilting is that not only can one make traditional quilts, but art quilts are in the scope of your possibilities. I enjoy creating art quilts because I am able to use unique fabrics, color and design to tell a story. I am able to relate the African American History stories. These quilts are an extension of the oral tradition which is characteristic of African culture. Historic events and people can be vividly related in fabric and stitches.

Education is a main attribute of the Kwanzaa celebration. This is a time to learn about family roots and to inspire the young to mark their paths and create their dreams. The Principle of Nia means Purpose therefore important stories should be told orally and with stitches. These quilts will be displayed and serve as a constant reminder of the pride of our culture. This art will honor those who have come before and left this glorious legacy."

Julius Bremer

Julius Bremer

"A narrative quilt gives the quilter such a wide world for seizing stories from African American historical events. These stories can be told by stitching words into the folds and pieces of every scrap. With today's fabric, use of color and texture, the heroes, sheroes and historical events will jump into your imagination. As an artist I want to inspire our youth to reach up to gather courage for their dreams."

Julius Bremer

Kwanzaa

Creativity is the key to my life. I enjoy the needle arts, such as, dressmaking, quilting, beading, soft sculpture, doll making, as well as hand and machine embroidery to name a few. Call me especially for doll making. This craft gives me an opportunity to use all of my skills to create lifelike dolls. Costuming the doll and teaching are also a part of my set of skills. I strive to find authentic cloth, beads, and accessories to present an accurate and interesting character of a doll.

I have won many awards for my dolls and quilts locally and nationally. You may have seen some of my work at:

The National Underground Railroad Freedom Center
Rock and Roll Hall of Fame, Cleveland, Ohio
North Chagrin Reservation Metro Park, Tripoint Hospital
Ursuline College
Cuyahoga Community College
The Artists Archives of the Western Reserve

Title: Kwanzaa
Artist: Myrya Johnson
Size: 31" X 46"
Year: 2018
Materials: Cotton, Polyester, Mixed Material

Myrya Johnson

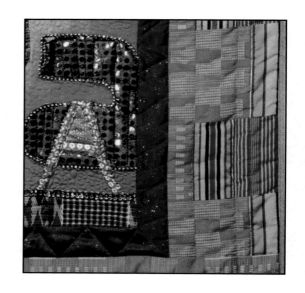

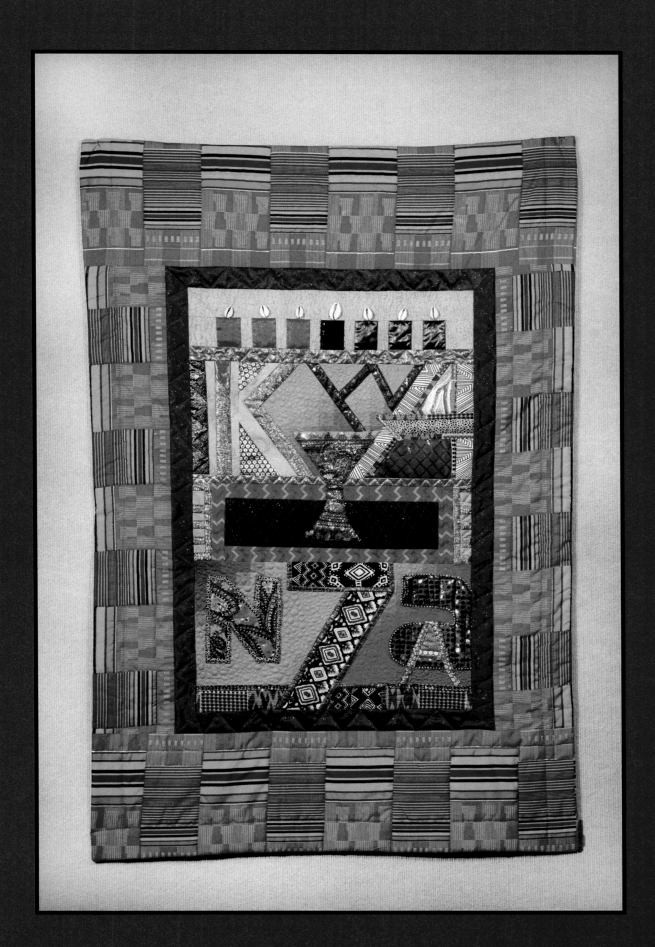

Elegantly Dressed Ladies

As an enthusiastic quilter, it is my mission to try new quilt patterns and techniques as I find them. I have been quilting for many years but the idea of using Kwanzaa as the theme for a quilt was new to me.

My family did not celebrate Kwanzaa until I joined our guild and learned more about its valuable foundation. Buying a new embroidery machine caused me to imagine the beautiful possibilities for my Kwanzaa quilt. I knew that I had to make a quilt that celebrated one of the traditions of this holiday. I wanted to stitch out the scene in my mind of the family members gathered together at the Karamu dressed in their traditional dresses, headwraps, dashikis, kufis, and suits. The colorful African designs and styles from various countries fascinated me. I could not always find the designs I wanted, but making this quilt was a joy to create.

Title: Elegantly Dressed Ladies
Artist: Sandra Moore
Size: 56" X 54"
Year: 2016

Materials: Cotton, Embroidery

Sandra Moore

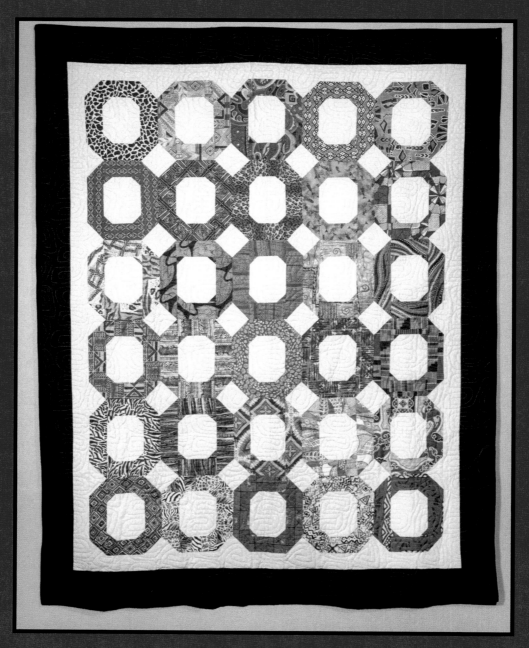

"There are so many quilt patterns that I would like to try, but the days are short and the designs and techniques are many. Symbols in textiles are fascinating to me because they can represent many ideas which set in textiles are useful. In quilting, geometric shapes are often pieced into design. Certain symbols have grown to mean a specific idea. Hearts mean love. Arrows show direction. The Underground Railroad quilt is made of a series of symbols. Symbols may give voiceless direction or secret education. Circles may symbolize continuity, unity, or commitment.

I created this quilt because of the circle pattern and how the entire quilt seemed to enhance the circle as a symbol of the Kwanzaa theme."

Sandra Moore

Sandra Moore

ZAWADI

Zawadi is a powerful and loving Kiswahili word which means "gift." Kwanzaa is a time for celebrating family love through giving a special kind of gift. Love in a family encourages demonstrations of gifts and kind acts. Therefore gift sharing would be more than appropriate for a family gathering at Kwanzaa.

During this African American celebration gifts are given especially to children, "the watoto." Handcrafted items are treasured. Dolls, books, quilts, wooden items given at this time are cherished forever. Handmade, thoughtfully appropriate gifts are encouraged. The zawadi could also be a promise to give time to others, to improve school work, or the setting down of positive personal goals for the year. Books are a special zawadi for this time. Setting personal goals is one of the main objectives of the Kwanzaa celebration for the entire family.

African dolls representing various areas of African culture, along with their stories and traditions are special treasures. Today there is a need for Black Dolls that look like and are complimentary to African American life. Our children need to see themselves in a favorable light.

Zawadi Dolls

Rosa Parks
Pamela Smith

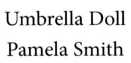

Umbrella Doll
Pamela Smith

Doll with Basket
Pamela Smith

Zawadi Dolls

Hope
Gloria Kellon

Doll on a Box
Myrya Johnson

Mudcloth Doll
Mary Pinckney

I Am Woman
Mary Pinckney

Black and White Doll
Mary Pinckney

Namibian Doll
Gloria Kellon

70

Zawadi Dolls

Jointed Doll
Myrya Johnson

Zawadi Doll
Priscilla Bradley

Danitra Brown Doll
Gloria Kellon

Doll in Chair
Myrya Johnson

Zawadi Dolls

Man with Trophy
Pamela Smith

Buffalo Soldier
Gloria Kellon

Bess Gates

Myrya Johnson

Zawadi Dolls
African Queens

Pamela Smith

Priscilla Bradley

South African Doll
Myrya Johnson

Aunt Jemima Doll
Myrya Johnson

Doll with Apron and Vegetables
Pamela Smith

Zawadi Dolls

Large Raggety Ann and Andy
Myrya Johnson

Small Raggety Ann Doll
Mary Pinckney

Zawadi Dolls

Raggety Ann and Andy
Myrya Johnson

Zawadi Doll Bag
Myrya Johnson

Kwanzaa Mama
Pillow Doll
Gloria Kellon

Zawadi Gifts

Kwanzaa Clock
Sandra Moore
Jacqueline Boyd

Tuffett
Jacqueline Boyd

Tuffett
Myrya Johnson

Two Dolls on a Purse
Myrya Johnson

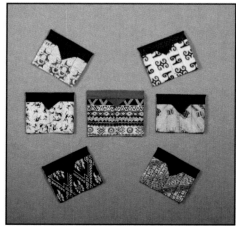

Zawadi Purses
Sandra Moore

Purse
Myrya Johnson

Made in the USA
Columbia, SC
25 May 2021